Take 5 Fat Quarters

15 EASY QUILT PATTERNS

Kathy Brown

D1561119

Martingale®
Create with Confidence

Dedication

For my husband and daughter.

I'm reminded of a quote I read one day by Michael J. Fox: *"Family is not an important thing, it is everything."*

My husband: you are my best friend, my confidant, my rock, and my shoulder through good times and bad. For 40 years and counting, you are my everything.

My daughter: you are my joy and the light of my life. Watching your journey into the confident, compassionate, intelligent, beautiful young woman that you are has been the most wonderful gift I could imagine. ILYBTTWS!

Take 5 Fat Quarters: 15 Easy Quilt Patterns
© 2014 by Kathy Brown

Martingale®
19021 120th Ave. NE, Ste. 102
Bothell, WA 98011-9511 USA
ShopMartingale.com

Printed in China

19 18 17 16 15 14   8 7 6 5 4 3 2 1

Library of Congress Cataloging-in-Publication Data is available upon request.

ISBN: 978-1-60468-417-9

Mission Statement

Dedicated to providing quality products and service to inspire creativity.

Credits

PUBLISHER AND CHIEF VISIONARY OFFICER: Jennifer Erbe Keltner

EDITOR IN CHIEF: Mary V. Green

DESIGN DIRECTOR: Paula Schlosser

MANAGING EDITOR: Karen Costello Soltys

ACQUISITIONS EDITOR: Karen M. Burns

TECHNICAL EDITOR: Laura Stone Roberts

COPY EDITOR: Melissa Bryan

PRODUCTION MANAGER: Regina Girard

COVER AND INTERIOR DESIGNER: Connor Chin

PHOTOGRAPHER: Brent Kane

ILLUSTRATOR: Anne Moscicki

Contents

Introduction

My early years were full of mom-isms that have remained with me throughout my life: "Close that door, you weren't born in a barn," "Two wrongs don't make a right," "Don't try to pull the wool over my eyes, I wasn't born yesterday," and other similar phrases that filled each day of my formative years. Some of these I took with a grain of salt, some I took to heart, and some I just plain did not understand, but there they were, planted in my brain for all eternity. One such mom-ism that has proven to rise up and bite me throughout my years, however, was one of my mom's favorites: "Never say 'never.'" Let's take a look at that one!

Back in 2005 when I created the pattern Take 5, I was proud of the fact that the quilt was not a fat-quarter pattern—proud that I had achieved the scrappy look normally associated with fat-quarter patterns, but that I had done so using five fabrics in varying yardages. From that single concept, a number of patterns and two books were created, all using five fabrics in various yardage amounts. For years, whenever someone would inquire whether any of the Take 5 patterns were or could be made with fat quarters, my response was always a resounding "No! They were not and would never be made with fat quarters." So there it was. I threw down the gauntlet time and time again, saying the words "no" and "never."

Until *that* night. *That* night when I woke from a sound sleep with the idea that maybe, just maybe, the Take 5 concept could be made with fat quarters. *Maybe* this could work. Maybe the quilts would be smaller in construction, like "Meet Me in the Middle" on page 13. Or maybe, if I added some neutral yardage as a filler or background in the quilt, as in "Spring Fling" on page 17 and "Crisscross Applesauce" on page 32, the quilts could grow a bit into lap-sized projects. And maybe, just *maybe*, the quilts could become *quite* ample in size like "Tranquillity" on page 57! Quilters could still choose five coordinating fabrics—they would all just be in fat-quarter form instead of yardage. Hmm, maybe I shouldn't have been so adamant with my "no's" and "nevers," because I began to believe that maybe, just *maybe*, this concept could work!

So I forged ahead, diving into my sizable stash of fat quarters and creating Take 5 quilts made with just five fat quarters (ahem—plus that little bit of added yardage here and there for those fillers and backgrounds)!

Which brings us to the present. Realizing that I was embarking on a totally different path with the Take 5 concept, I had to mend my ways. Yes, I had to admit that I was wrong, and that I should *never* have uttered the word *never*, because I did find a way to make scrappy-looking quilts with just five fat quarters! And so a new series of Take 5 quilts was born.

For those of you who have loved all of the Take 5 quilt patterns and *Take 5* and *More Take 5* books, I'm sure you're going to embrace these new quilts with just as much fun and enthusiasm as I have. For those of you who haven't yet had the chance to make a Take 5 quilt, now is your chance with this group of quilts that use fat quarters! Run to your stash or hop in the car for a quick trip to your local quilt shop, choose five fat quarters, and get quilting!

A Step in the Right Direction

designed by Kathy Brown, pieced by Linda Reed, quilted by Carol Hilton

Destined to always try to please, to always do the right thing, I was pretty much a rule follower in my formative years. No matter what task I took on, I tried to do it to the best of my ability. I remember my dad watching over me one Christmas when I commandeered my brothers' erector set and proceeded to build something I considered very intricate and challenging! During that process I became quite frustrated, and I can still hear Dad's calming voice repeating several times that I shouldn't worry—I was taking a step in the right direction. I don't recall what that monstrosity eventually ended up being that day, but I do remember my dad's reassuring comment resonating over and over in my head. To this day, whenever I'm faced with a difficult task, I remind myself that every step I take forward is a step in the right direction.

As this quilt was taking shape, the short and long step pattern that formed in the design reminded me of Dad's calming words. So, what direction will you choose to take with this quilt?

Finished quilt: 40½" x 52½"
Finished block: 6" x 6"

Materials

Yardage is based on 42"-wide fabric. Fat quarters measure 18" x 21".

1 fat quarter *each* of 5 assorted tan and red prints for blocks

1½ yards of tan-and-red floral for outer border and binding

1¼ yards of red tone on tone for background and inner border

3 yards of fabric for backing

49" x 61" piece of batting

Cutting the Fat Quarters

To cut the fat quarters efficiently, lay them all right side up, one on top of the other in a uniform stack (see "Rotary Cutting" on page 61). Trim the left and bottom edges of the stack to square them up. Refer to the cutting diagram below to cut the layered fabrics as indicated.

From *each* tan-and-red fat quarter, cut:
  4 strips, 2½" x 21"; crosscut into:
    14 squares, 2½" x 2½" (70 total)
    7 rectangles, 2½" x 4½" (35 total)

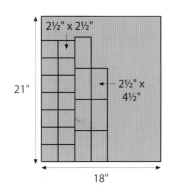

Cutting the Remaining Pieces

From the red tone on tone, cut:
  9 strips, 2½" x 42"; crosscut into 70 rectangles, 2½" x 4½"
  11 strips, 1½" x 42"; crosscut *5 of the strips* into 70 rectangles, 1½" x 2½"

From the tan-and-red floral, cut:
  8 strips, 4½" x 42"
  5 strips, 2½" x 42"

Constructing the Blocks

All the blocks are made in the same manner. Press the seam allowances as indicated by the arrows in the diagrams.

1. With right sides together, sew a tan print 2½" square to a red tone-on-tone 2½" x 4½" rectangle. Make two matching units.

2. With right sides together, sew a red tone-on-tone 1½" x 2½" rectangle to each end of a matching tan print 2½" x 4½" rectangle.

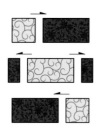

3. Sew the units from step 1 to the top and bottom of the unit from step 2 to complete the block. Make seven matching blocks.

4. Repeat steps 1–3 to make seven blocks from each of the remaining fat-quarter prints, for a total of 35 blocks.

Make 7 of each print
(35 total).

Assembling the Quilt Top

1. Using a design wall or other flat surface, arrange the completed blocks in seven rows of five blocks each, with the like-fabric blocks forming a step pattern as shown above right.

2. Sew the blocks into rows, pressing the seam allowances in opposite directions from row to row. Sew the rows together to form the quilt top.

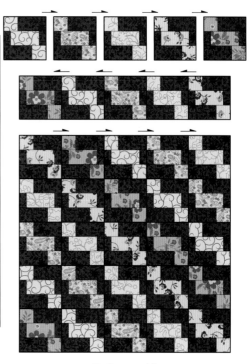

Quilt assembly

3. Referring to "Adding Borders" on page 62, sew two red tone-on-tone 1½" x 42" strips together to make one long strip; make two. Stitch the strips to the sides of the quilt top, and then trim the excess even with the top and bottom of the quilt top. Press the seam allowances toward the border strips. Sew the remaining red tone-on-tone 1½" x 42" strips to the top and bottom of the quilt. Trim the excess even with the sides of the quilt top. Press the seam allowances toward the strips.

4. Sew two floral 4½"-wide strips together to make one long strip. Repeat to make four long strips. Sew the strips to the quilt top for the outer border. Press.

Finishing

1. Refer to "Completing the Quilt" on page 62 to layer the quilt top, batting, and backing. Quilt as desired.

2. Sew the floral 2½"-wide strips together to form one continuous strip and use it to bind the quilt.

Staying Focused

designed by Kathy Brown, pieced by Linda Reed, quilted by Carol Hilton

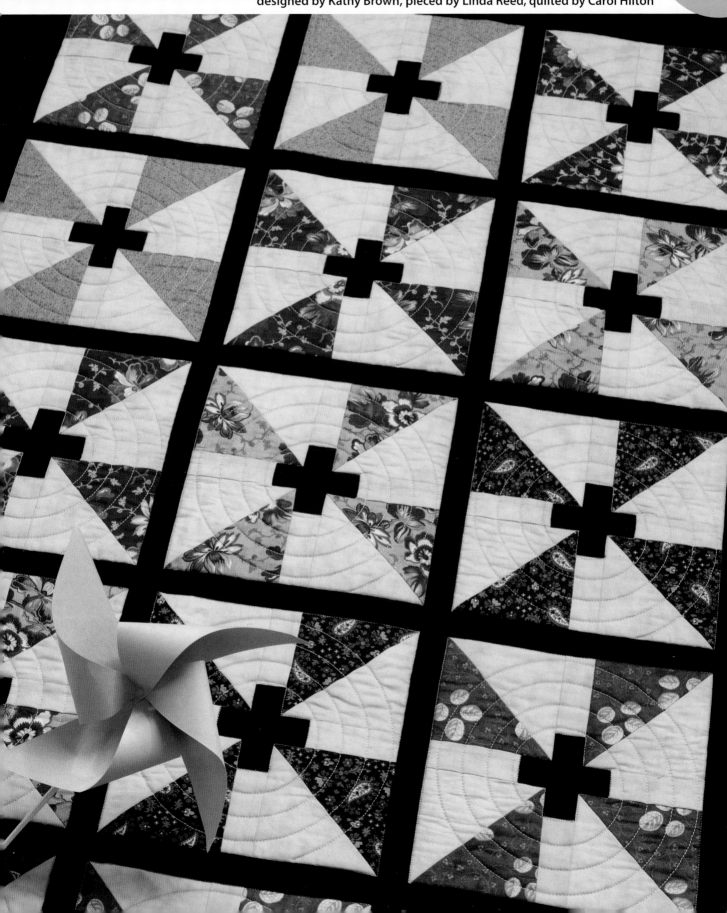

I am a right-brained person—a dreamer who is always creating, enjoying life and all it has to offer, never worrying about or focusing on the analytical, everyday details. Those traits tended to carry over into my schoolwork as I was growing up, and my teachers in those years reminded me that I had to stay focused on the tasks at hand when my mind would wander and take me to places and things I would have much rather been doing.

As I was working on this quilt design, the words of my former educators rang sharp and clear in my head! The pinwheels are symbolic of my mind, turning and spinning with new ideas and creative endeavors, while the cross in the center is the ever-mindful symbol reminding me to come back to reality and stay focused. It's that balance between the crazy spinning and the static center cross that formed the design of this quilt, and it suits my personality perfectly.

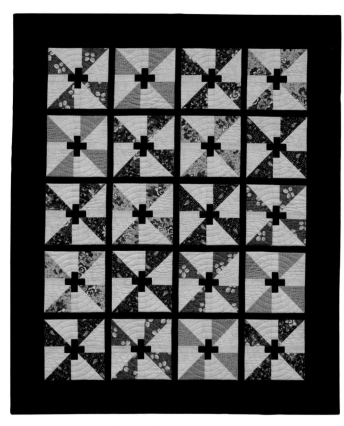

Finished quilt: 49½" x 59½"
Finished block: 9" x 9"

Materials

Yardage is based on 42"-wide fabric. Fat quarters measure 18" x 21".

1 fat quarter *each* of red, gold, green, blue, and black florals for blocks

2⅜ yards of black solid for blocks, sashing, border, and binding

1¼ yards of light-tan solid for blocks

3½ yards of fabric for backing

58" x 68" piece of batting

Cutting the Layered Fat Quarters

To cut the fat quarters efficiently, lay them all right side up, one on top of the other in a uniform stack (see "Rotary Cutting" on page 61). Trim the left and bottom edges of the stack to square them up. Refer to the cutting diagram below to cut the layered fabrics as indicated.

From *each* fat quarter, cut:
2 strips, 5" x 21"; crosscut into 8 squares, 5" x 5" (40 total)

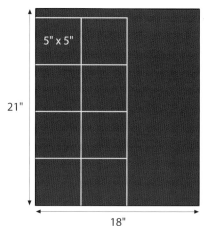

Cutting the Remaining Pieces

From the light-tan solid, cut:
  5 strips, 5" x 42"; crosscut into 40 squares, 5" x 5"
  8 strips, 1½" x 42"; crosscut into 80 strips,
    1½" x 3½"

From the black solid, cut:
  8 strips, 1½" x 42"; crosscut into:
    40 squares, 1½" x 1½"
    20 strips, 1½" x 3½"
    15 strips, 1½" x 9½"
  4 strips, 1½" x 39½"
  8 strips, 5½" x 42"
  6 strips, 2½" x 42"

Constructing the Blocks

All the blocks are made in the same manner. Press the seam allowances as indicated by the arrows in the diagrams.

1. Draw a diagonal line from corner to corner on the wrong side of the tan 5" squares.

2. Place a marked square right sides together with a floral 5" square. Sew ¼" from the marked line on each side. Cut on the drawn line to yield two half-square-triangle units. Repeat to make 16 half-square-triangle units from *each* of the five floral fabrics. Trim the units to measure 4½" x 4½".

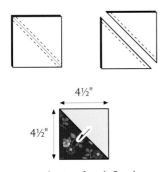

Make 16 of each floral
(80 total).

3. Sew a black 1½" square to one end of a tan 1½" x 3½" strip to make a short pieced strip. Repeat to make 40 short pieced strips.

Make 40.

4. Sew a tan 1½" x 3½" strip to each end of a black 1½" x 3½" strip to make a long pieced strip. Repeat to make 20 long pieced strips.

Make 20.

5. Sew matching half-square-triangle units to opposite sides of a short pieced strip to make a row; make two. Be sure to orient the units and strips as shown. Sew the rows to opposite sides of a long pieced strip to complete the block. Make four matching blocks. Repeat to make four blocks from each of the remaining floral fabrics, for a total of 20 blocks.

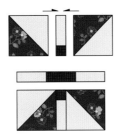 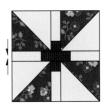

Make 4 of each color
(20 total).

Assembling the Quilt Top

1. Using a design wall or other flat surface, arrange the completed blocks in five rows of four blocks and three black 1½" x 9½" sashing strips each as shown in the quilt assembly diagram on page 12.

2. Sew the blocks and sashing strips into rows, and press the seam allowances toward the strips. Sew the rows and the black 1½" x 39½" sashing strips together to form the quilt top. Press the seam allowances toward the strips.

3. Referring to "Adding Borders" on page 62, sew two black 5½"-wide strips together to make one long strip. Repeat to make four long strips. Sew two of the strips to the sides of the quilt

top, and then trim the excess even with the top and bottom of the quilt top. Press the seam allowances toward the border strips. Sew the remaining long strips to the top and bottom of the quilt. Trim the excess even with the sides of the quilt top. Press the seam allowances toward the strips.

Finishing

1. Refer to "Completing the Quilt" on page 62 to layer the quilt top, batting, and backing. Quilt as desired.

2. Sew the black 2½"-wide strips together to form one continuous strip and use it to bind the quilt.

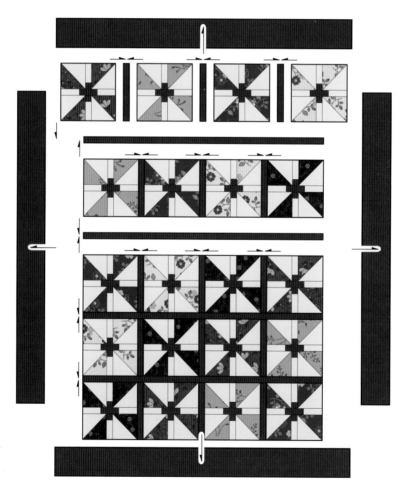

Quilt assembly

Meet Me in the Middle

designed by Kathy Brown, pieced by Linda Reed, quilted by Carol Hilton

Teaching first grade many years ago was both a delight and a challenge. Many times I found myself in the position of wanting to follow the rules dictated by the administration, but emotionally torn by also wanting to challenge those rules when I was certain that the end result would be a more rewarding outcome for a student. It was my job to be an advocate for those students, convince the administration that my challenge was justified, and somehow have everyone "meet in the middle" toward a solution.

Working on this quilt, with all of the different fabrics surrounding those blocks in the middle, reminded me of one of those times, and of a happy ending for a little six-year-old boy who will forever remain in my heart! Henry, this quilt is for you!

Finished quilt: 33½" x 43½"
Finished block: 4½" x 5½"

Materials

Yardage is based on 42"-wide fabric. Fat quarters measure 18" x 21".

1 fat quarter *each* of red, gold, gray, green, and brown prints for blocks and binding

1⅓ yards of brown solid for blocks, sashing, and border

1⅝ yards of fabric for backing

42" x 52" piece of batting

Cutting the Fat Quarters

To cut the red, gold, gray, and green fat quarters efficiently, lay them all right side up, one on top of the other in a uniform stack (see "Rotary Cutting" on page 61). Trim the left and bottom edges of the stack to square them up. Refer to the cutting diagrams on page 15 to cut the layered fabrics and the brown fat quarter as indicated.

From each red, gold, gray, and green fat quarter, cut:
    1 strip, 5" x 21"; crosscut into 3 squares, 5" x 5" (12 total)
    2 strips, 2½" x 21" (8 total)

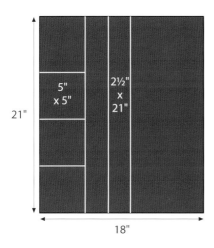

From the brown fat quarter, cut:
    3 strips, 4½" x 21"; crosscut into 11 squares, 4½" x 4½"
    1 strip, 2½" x 21"

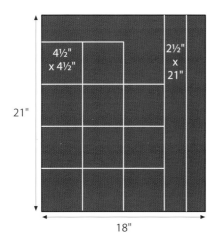

Cutting the Remaining Pieces

From the brown solid, cut:
    2 strips, 5" x 42"; crosscut into 12 squares, 5" x 5"
    4 strips, 1½" x 42"; crosscut into 30 strips, 1½" x 4½"
    4 strips, 1½" x 34½"
    4 strips, 5" x 42"

Constructing the Blocks

All the blocks are made in the same manner. Press the seam allowances as indicated by the arrows in the diagrams.

1. With a light-colored chalk pencil, draw a diagonal line from corner to corner on the wrong side of the brown-solid 5" squares.

2. Place a marked square right sides together with a red, gold, gray, or green 5" square. Sew ¼" from the marked line on each side. Cut on the drawn line to yield two half-square-triangle units. Repeat to make six units from *each* of the red, gold, gray, and green prints. Trim the units to measure 4½" x 4½".

Make 6 of each color (24 total).

3. Orienting the half-square-triangle units as shown, sew a brown-solid 1½" x 4½" strip to the bottom of each of the units as shown to complete a block. Two each of the blue and green units will not have a brown strip added. In the same manner, sew a brown-solid 1½" x 4½" strip to the bottom of 10 of the brown-print 4½" squares to complete the blocks. Make 30 blocks total.

Make 6.   Make 6.   Make 4.   Make 4.   Make 10.

Assembling the Quilt Top

1. Using a design wall or other flat surface, arrange the completed blocks in five vertical columns of six blocks plus one unit or square each as shown in the quilt assembly diagram.

2. Sew the blocks into columns. Sew the columns and the brown 1½" x 34½" sashing strips together to form the quilt top.

3. Referring to "Adding Borders" on page 62, stitch two brown 5"-wide strips to the sides of the quilt top, and then trim the excess even with the top and bottom of the quilt top. Press the seam allowances toward the border strips.

Sew the remaining brown strips to the top and bottom of the quilt. Trim the excess even with the sides of the quilt top. Press the seam allowances toward the strips.

Finishing

1. Refer to "Completing the Quilt" on page 62 to layer the quilt top, batting, and backing. Quilt as desired.

2. Sew the red, gold, green, gray, and brown 2½"-wide strips together, alternating colors, to form one continuous strip and use it to bind the quilt.

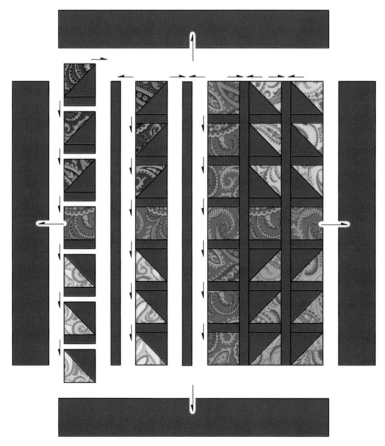

Quilt assembly

Spring Fling

designed by Kathy Brown, pieced by Linda Reed, quilted by Carol Hilton

*H*aving lived in Louisiana all my life, I'm accustomed to the heat and humidity that pervades our climate 90 percent of the time. So when the first hint of spring rolls around, and the cool temperatures and low humidity are present for a short couple of weeks, my heart rejoices! I love not only the feel of the air that comes with that special time, but the abundance of spring greens and crystal-blue skies that accompany the cooler temperatures and bright, sunny days.

Walking into my local quilt shop on a very hot and humid summer day, I was greeted by brand-new bolts of the lovely batiks that are showcased in this quilt. They instantly reminded me of the bright sunshine, blue skies, and fresh new greens associated with our rare spring days. Knowing I had to make a quilt in celebration of those precious days of springtime, I was thrilled to find fabrics that were perfect for just such a quilt—a spring fling in the making!

Finished quilt: 61½" x 74½"
Finished block: 12" x 12"

Materials

Yardage is based on 42"-wide fabric. Fat quarters measure 18" x 21".

1 fat quarter *each* of 5 different turquoise and green batiks for blocks

3⅝ yards of yellow-and-turquoise print batik for blocks, outer border, and binding

2 yards of white solid for blocks, sashing, and inner border

4⅓ yards of fabric for backing

70" x 83" piece of batting

Cutting the Layered Fat Quarters

To cut the fat quarters efficiently, lay them all right side up, one on top of the other in a uniform stack (see "Rotary Cutting" on page 61). Trim the left and bottom edges of the stack to square them up. Refer to the cutting diagram below to cut the layered fabrics as indicated.

From *each* fat quarter, cut:
6 strips, 2½" x 21"; crosscut into:
16 squares, 2½" x 2½" (80 total)
16 strips, 2½" x 4½" (80 total)

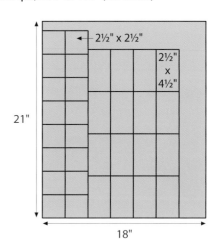

Cutting the Remaining Pieces

From the white solid, cut:
  10 strips, 2½" x 42"; crosscut into 160 squares, 2½" x 2½"
  3 strips, 3" x 42"; crosscut into 40 squares, 3" x 3"
  21 strips, 1½" x 42"; crosscut *5 of the strips* into 15 strips, 1½" x 12½"

From the yellow-and-turquoise print batik, cut:
  19 strips, 2½" x 42"; crosscut into:
    40 strips, 2½" x 12½"
    40 strips, 2½" x 4½"
  4 strips, 3" x 42"; crosscut into 40 squares, 3" x 3"
  8 strips, 4½" x 42"
  8 strips, 2½" x 42"

Constructing the Blocks

All the blocks are made in the same manner. Press the seam allowances as indicated by the arrows in the diagrams.

1. Sew a white 2½" square to the right edge of a green 2½" square and then add a green 2½" x 4½" strip to the top. Repeat to make four matching units.

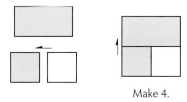

Make 4.

2. Draw a diagonal line from corner to corner on the wrong side of two white 3" squares.

3. Place a marked square right sides together with a yellow 3" square. Sew ¼" from the marked line on each side. Cut on the drawn line to yield two half-square-triangle units. Repeat to make four half-square-triangle units. Trim the units to measure 2½" x 2½".

Make 4.

4. Sew two half-square-triangle units together, orienting them as shown; press. Sew to one long edge of a yellow 2½" x 4½" strip. Repeat to make two units.

Make 2.

5. Draw a diagonal line from corner to corner on the wrong side of four white 2½" squares. Place a marked square on one end of a yellow 2½" x 12½" strip, right sides together with the line angled in the direction shown. Sew on the drawn line. Trim the excess fabric ¼" from the sewn line, fold back the triangle, and press. Repeat on the opposite end of the strip. Repeat to make two strip units.

     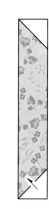

Make 2.

6. Sew two units from step 1 to opposite sides of a unit from step 4. Press. Repeat to make two units.

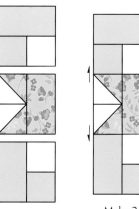

Make 2.

7. Sew a unit from step 6 to the left edge of a strip unit from step 5. Repeat to make a second unit. Sew the two units together to complete the block. Repeat steps 1–7 to make four blocks of each fat-quarter fabric, for a total of 20 blocks.

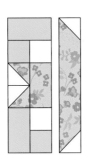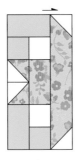

Make 2.

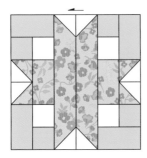

Make 4 of each fabric
(20 total).

Assembling the Quilt Top

1. Using a design wall or other flat surface, arrange the completed blocks in five rows of four blocks and three white 1½" x 12½" sashing strips each as shown above right.

2. Sew the blocks and sashing strips into rows, pressing the seam allowances toward the sashing strips. Sew two white 1½" x 42" strips together to make one long strip. Repeat to make eight long strips. Trim four of these strips to 51½" in length for sashing. Sew the rows and the white sashing strips together to form the quilt top.

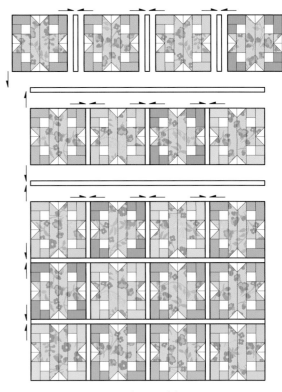

Quilt assembly

3. Referring to "Adding Borders" on page 62, sew two of the remaining long white strips to the sides of the quilt top, and then trim the excess even with the top and bottom of the quilt top. Press the seam allowances toward the border strips. Sew the remaining long white strips to the top and bottom of the quilt. Trim the excess even with the sides of the quilt top. Press the seam allowances toward the strips.

4. Sew two yellow 4½"-wide strips together to make one long strip. Repeat to make four long strips. Sew the strips to the quilt top for the outer border. Press.

Finishing

1. Refer to "Completing the Quilt" on page 62 to layer the quilt top, batting, and backing. Quilt as desired.

2. Sew the remaining yellow 2½"-wide strips together to form one continuous strip and use it to bind the quilt.

Swimming the Sidestroke

designed by Kathy Brown, pieced by Linda Reed, quilted by Carol Hilton

*O*h my, how I've always loved the water, be it the swimming pool, a lake, or the ocean. I guess it's a good thing my mother enrolled my brothers and me in summer swimming classes when we were very young. We took lessons for several years, advancing through the classes and learning increasingly difficult strokes and techniques. But no matter how much we advanced, and how strong we were in the water, we always followed Mom's rule of "You can't go swimming for an hour after you eat. You'll get cramps and drown!" I think I believed that one until I was in my late teens.

When I put the blocks together in this quilt design, they instantly reminded me of my meandering ways in the water, looking like colorful little swimsuits heading left and heading right. This colorful quilt is sure to delight!

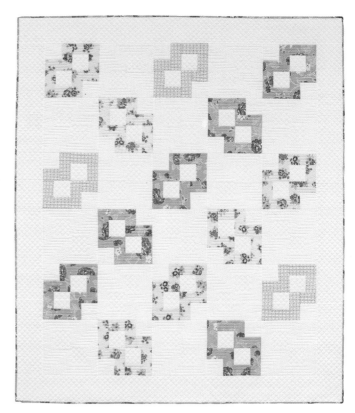

Finished quilt: 60½" x 70½"
Finished block: 10" x 10"

Materials

Yardage is based on 42"-wide fabric. Fat quarters measure 18" x 21".

1 fat quarter *each* of yellow, aqua, green, orange, and pink florals for blocks

3⅔ yards of white solid for blocks and border

⅝ yard of melon-orange print for binding

4⅛ yards of fabric for backing

69" x 79" piece of batting

Cutting the Layered Fat Quarters

To cut the fat quarters efficiently, lay them all right side up, one on top of the other in a uniform stack (see "Rotary Cutting" on page 61). Trim the left and bottom edges of the stack to square them up. Refer to the cutting diagram below to cut the layered fabrics as indicated.

From *each* fat quarter, cut:

2 strips, 3½" x 21"; crosscut into 12 rectangles, 2½" x 3½" (60 total)

3 strips, 2½" x 21"; crosscut into 12 rectangles, 2½" x 5½" (60 total)

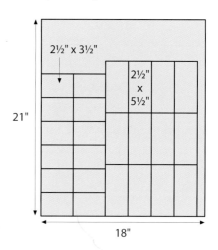

Cutting the Remaining Pieces

From the white solid, cut:
  6 strips, 3½" x 42"; crosscut into 60 squares, 3½" x 3½"
  5 strips, 10½" x 42"; crosscut into 15 squares, 10½" x 10½"
  8 strips, 5½" x 42"

From the melon-orange print, cut:
  7 strips, 2½" x 42"

Constructing the Blocks

All the blocks are made in the same manner. Press the seam allowances as indicated by the arrows in the diagrams.

1. With right sides together, sew a yellow 2½" x 3½" rectangle to the bottom of a white 3½" square. Add a yellow 2½" x 5½" rectangle to the right edge to make a unit. Repeat to make 12 units from *each* of the five floral fabrics.

Make 12 of each floral
(60 total).

2. Orient four matching units as shown. Sew two units together to make a row; make two. Sew the rows together to complete a block. Repeat to make three blocks from each of the five floral fabrics, for a total of 15 blocks.

 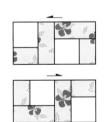

Make 3 of each floral
(15 total).

Assembling the Quilt Top

1. Using a design wall or other flat surface, arrange the completed blocks and white 10½" squares into six rows as shown in the quilt assembly diagram.

2. Sew the blocks and squares into rows, and press the seam allowances toward the white squares. Sew the rows together and press the seam allowances in one direction.

3. Referring to "Adding Borders" on page 62, sew two white 5½"-wide strips together to make one long strip. Repeat to make four long strips. Stitch two of the strips to the sides of the quilt top, and then trim the excess even with the top and bottom of the quilt top. Press the seam allowances toward the border strips. Sew the remaining long strips to the top and bottom of the quilt. Trim the excess even with the sides of the quilt top. Press the seam allowances toward the strips.

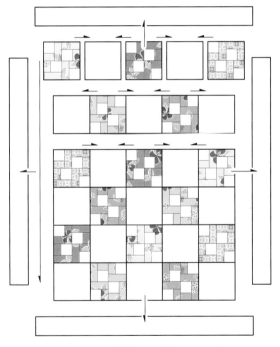

Quilt assembly

Finishing

1. Refer to "Completing the Quilt" on page 62 to layer the quilt top, batting, and backing. Quilt as desired.

2. Sew the melon-orange 2½"-wide strips together to form one continuous strip and use it to bind the quilt.

Upstairs, Downstairs

designed by Kathy Brown, pieced by Linda Reed, quilted by Carol Hilton

When I was young, my paternal grandparents lived in an upstairs apartment on a lake near the campus of Louisiana State University. This locale was the perfect solution for my grandfather, a professor at the university, since he didn't own a car and could walk the few blocks to campus every day. As a small child, I loved walking up and down the polished oak staircase to reach their apartment. When I close my eyes, I can remember the cool, heavy stucco walls that embraced the staircase in contrast to the dark, smooth stairs that I climbed.

The blocks in this quilt remind me of that apartment long ago and how I used to navigate that staircase to reach the loving arms of my grandparents. Perhaps these blocks might spark a memory of your own and you will make your personalized version of "Upstairs, Downstairs"!

Finished quilt: 48½" x 64½"
Finished block: 8" x 8"

Materials

Yardage is based on 42"-wide fabric. Fat quarters measure 18" x 21".

1 fat quarter *each* of 5 assorted orange prints for blocks

3 yards of white solid for blocks and border

⅝ yard of orange mottled print for binding

3½ yards of fabric for backing

57" x 73" piece of batting

Cutting the Layered Fat Quarters

To cut the fat quarters efficiently in stacks of two or three as indicated, lay them right side up, one on top of the other in a uniform stack (see "Rotary Cutting" on page 61). Trim the left and bottom edges of the stack to square them up. Refer to the cutting diagrams at right and on page 26 to cut the layered fabrics as indicated.

From *each of 3* fat quarters, cut:
5 strips, 2½" x 21"; crosscut into:
    4 strips, 2½" x 8½" (12 total)
    4 strips, 2½" x 6½" (12 total)
    4 strips, 2½" x 4½" (12 total)
    4 squares, 2½" x 2½" (12 total)

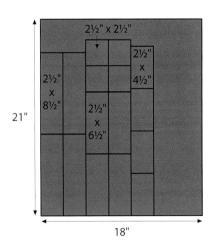

From *each* of the *remaining 2* fat quarters, cut:
  4 strips, 2½" x 21"; crosscut into:
    3 strips, 2½" x 8½" (6 total)
    3 strips, 2½" x 6½" (6 total)
    3 strips, 2½" x 4½" (6 total)
    3 squares, 2½" x 2½" (6 total)

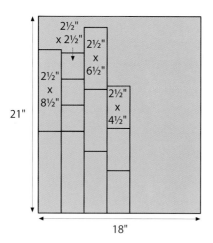

Cutting the Remaining Pieces

From the white solid, cut:
  8 strips, 2½" x 42"; crosscut into:
    18 strips, 2½" x 6½"
    18 strips, 2½" x 4½"
    18 squares, 2½" x 2½"
  5 strips, 8½" x 42"; crosscut into 17 squares,
    8½" x 8½"
  8 strips, 4½" x 42"

From the orange mottled print, cut:
  7 strips, 2½" x 42"

Constructing the Blocks

Each block is sewn using a single orange print plus the white solid. All of the orange prints are used in both A blocks (right-facing) and B blocks (left-facing). Press the seam allowances as indicated by the arrows in the diagrams.

1. With right sides together, sew an orange 2½" square to the left end of a white 6½" strip. Sew an orange 4½" strip to the left end of a white 4½" strip. Sew an orange 6½" strip to the left side of a white 2½" square.

2. Sew the pieced strips from step 1 together as shown, and then sew an orange 8½" strip to the bottom to complete one A block. Repeat to make 12 total A blocks in assorted orange prints.

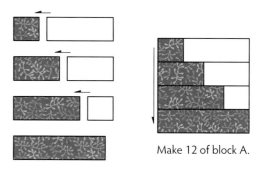

Make 12 of block A.

3. With right sides together, sew an orange 2½" square to the right end of a white 6½" strip. Sew an orange 4½" strip to the right end of a white 4½" strip. Sew an orange 6½" strip to the right side of a white 2½" square.

4. Sew the pieced strips from step 3 together as shown, and then sew an orange 8½" strip to the bottom to complete one B block. Repeat to make six total B blocks in assorted orange prints.

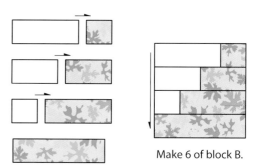

Make 6 of block B.

Assembling the Quilt Top

1. Using a design wall or other flat surface, arrange the completed blocks and white 8½" squares into seven rows as shown in the quilt assembly diagram.

2. Sew the blocks and squares into rows, pressing the seam allowances toward the white squares. Sew the rows together to form the quilt top. Press the seam allowances in one direction.

3. Referring to "Adding Borders" on page 62, sew two white 4½"-wide strips together to make one long strip. Repeat to make four long strips. Stitch two of the strips to the sides of the quilt top, and then trim the excess even with the top and bottom of the quilt top. Press the seam allowances toward the border strips. Sew the remaining long strips to the top and bottom of the quilt. Trim the excess even with the sides of the quilt top. Press the seam allowances toward the strips.

Finishing

1. Refer to "Completing the Quilt" on page 62 to layer the quilt top, batting, and backing. Quilt as desired.

2. Sew the orange 2½"-wide strips together to form one continuous strip and use it to bind the quilt.

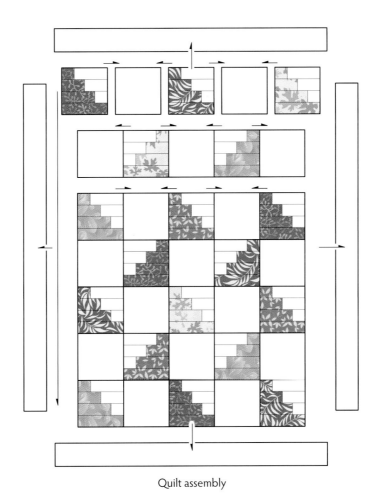

Quilt assembly

Rocky Mountain Memories

designed by Kathy Brown, pieced by Linda Reed, quilted by Carol Hilton

A business trip years ago offered me the opportunity to visit the lovely mountainous state of Colorado—quite a treat for a gal who lives at sea level! After a day filled with meetings, a group of us made the trek from Denver to Breckenridge for dinner. Along that scenic ride, I was fortunate enough to see many firsts in my life: buffalo grazing in pastures, elk on the side of the mountains, marmots scampering around the trails, and the simplicity of split-rail fences among the Colorado wildflowers. These sights were so beautiful, and I treasure the memories.

As I gathered the fabrics for this quilt, I was reminded of that experience and chose the fabrics with the sights I had seen in mind. The crystal-clear blue mountain lakes, the green pastures, brown split-rail fences and buffalo, and the fiery red of the setting sun over the mountains all came into focus with these fabrics. I hope you enjoy my version of a Colorado split-rail fence!

Finished quilt: 36½" x 48½"
Finished block: 6" x 6"

Materials

Yardage is based on 42"-wide fabric. Fat quarters measure 18" x 21".

1 fat quarter *each* of blue, green, brown, and red prints for blocks

1 fat quarter of gold print for flange

1¼ yards of cream floral for border and binding

⅜ yard of cream print for blocks

1¾ yards of fabric for backing*

44" x 56" piece of batting

If your backing fabric isn't 44" wide, you may need more than one width. If so, purchase 2⅞ yards of fabric for backing.

Cutting the Fat Quarters

To cut the blue, green, brown, and red fat quarters efficiently, lay them all right side up, one on top of the other in a uniform stack (see "Rotary Cutting" on page 61). Trim the left and bottom edges of the stack to square them up. Refer to the cutting diagrams on page 30 to cut the layered fabrics and the gold fat quarter as indicated.

From *each* blue, green, brown, and red fat quarter, cut:

4 strips, 2½" x 21"; crosscut into 24 rectangles, 2½" x 3½" (96 total)

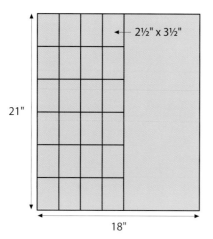

From the gold fat quarter, cut:

8 strips, 1½" x 21"

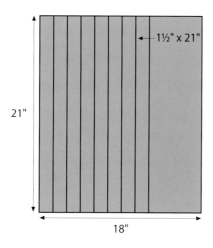

Cutting the Remaining Pieces

From the cream print, cut:

4 strips, 2½" x 42"; crosscut into 24 strips, 2½" x 6½"

From the cream floral, cut:

4 strips, 6½" x 42"
5 strips, 2½" x 42"

Constructing the Blocks

All the blocks are made in the same manner. Press the seam allowances as indicated by the arrows in the diagrams.

1. With right sides together, sew a red rectangle to a brown rectangle along the short edges. In the same manner, sew a blue rectangle to a green rectangle.

2. Orienting the step 1 units as shown, sew them to opposite sides of a cream-print 2½" x 6½" strip to complete the block. Repeat to make 24 blocks.

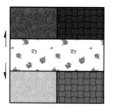

Make 24.

Assembling the Quilt Top

1. Using a design wall or other flat surface, arrange the completed blocks into six rows of four blocks each as shown below.

2. Sew the blocks into rows, pressing the seam allowances in opposite directions from row to row. Sew the rows together to form the quilt top. Press the seam allowances in one direction.

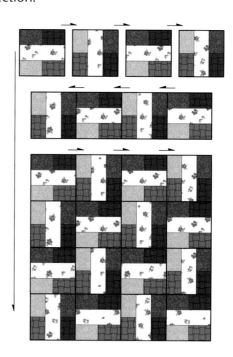

3. To make the flat gold piping, sew two gold 1½" x 21" strips together to make one long strip. Repeat to make four long strips. Fold the strips in half lengthwise, *wrong* sides together, and press.

4. With the fold toward the center of the quilt top and raw edges aligned, center one folded strip on the left side of the quilt top. Sew the strip in place, and then trim the excess length. Repeat on the opposite side of the quilt, and then on the top and bottom. Press flat, with the folded edges still toward the quilt center.

5. Referring to "Adding Borders" on page 62, stitch two of the floral 6½"-wide strips to the sides of the quilt top, and then trim the excess even with the top and bottom of the quilt top. Press the seam allowances toward the border strips. Sew the remaining floral 6½"-wide strips to the top and bottom of the quilt. Trim the excess even with the sides of the quilt top. Press the seam allowances toward the strips.

Finishing

1. Refer to "Completing the Quilt" on page 62 to layer the quilt top, batting, and backing. Quilt as desired.

2. Sew the floral 2½"-wide strips together to form one continuous strip and use it to bind the quilt.

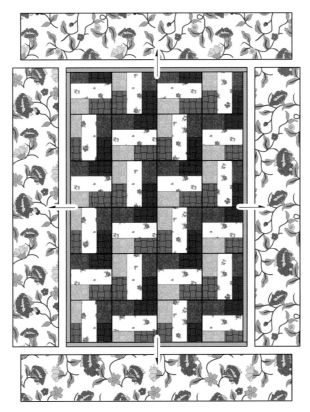

Quilt assembly

Crisscross Applesauce

designed by Kathy Brown, pieced by Linda Reed, quilted by Carol Hilton

M ost often when I am designing a quilt, the name of the quilt will come about because something in the fabrics or the design itself sparks a memory, and I then name the quilt appropriately for one of those inspirations. With this quilt, however, the exact opposite took place! A quick stop at my local public library had me glancing at a group of young children getting ready for story time. As I passed their area, the librarian was instructing them to sit in a circle, "crisscross applesauce"! Hearing that age-old phrase that I uttered many times myself as a child, I knew I had to design a quilt with that same name.

Here's to many days as a young child, sitting with legs crossed—crisscross applesauce—and the joy of discovering that some things never change!

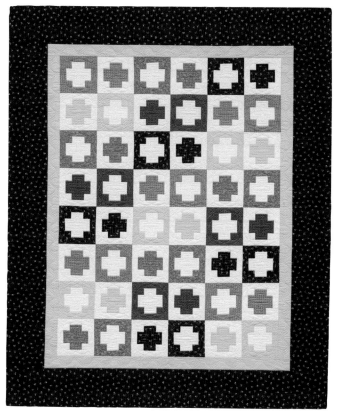

Finished quilt: 52½" x 64½"
Finished block: 6" x 6"

Materials

Yardage is based on 42"-wide fabric. Fat quarters measure 18" x 21".

1 fat quarter *each* of green, red, black, gold, and brown prints for blocks

2⅛ yards of black print for outer border and binding

1⅛ yards of cream solid for blocks

½ yard of gold tone on tone for inner border

3¾ yards of fabric for backing

61" x 73" piece of batting

Cutting the Fat Quarters

To cut the green, red, black, and gold fat quarters efficiently, lay them all right side up, one on top of the other in a uniform stack (see "Rotary Cutting" on page 61). Trim the left and bottom edges of the stack to square them up. Refer to the cutting diagrams at right and on page 34 to cut the layered fabrics and the brown fat quarter as indicated.

From *each* green, red, black, and gold fat quarter, cut:

4 strips, 1½" x 21"; crosscut into 30 rectangles, 1½" x 2½" (120 total)

4 strips, 2½" x 21"; crosscut into:
20 squares, 2½" x 2½" (80 total)
5 rectangles, 2½" x 4½" (20 total)

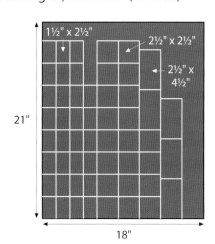

From the brown fat quarter, cut:
  3 strips, 1½" x 21"; crosscut into 24 rectangles, 1½" x 2½"
  3 strips, 2½" x 21"; crosscut into:
    16 squares, 2½" x 2½"
    4 rectangles, 2½" x 4½"

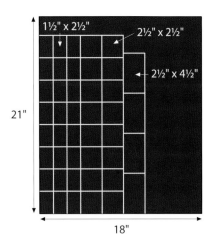

Cutting the Remaining Pieces

From the cream solid, cut:
  9 strips, 1½" x 42"; crosscut into 144 rectangles, 1½" x 2½"
  9 strips, 2½" x 42"; crosscut into:
    24 rectangles, 2½" x 4½"
    96 squares, 2½" x 2½"

From the gold tone on tone, cut:
  6 strips, 2½" x 42"

From the black print, cut:
  8 strips, 6½" x 42"
  7 strips, 2½" x 42"

Constructing the Blocks

All the blocks are made in the same manner. Press the seam allowances as indicated by the arrows in the diagrams.

1. With right sides together, sew a print 1½" x 2½" rectangle to a cream 1½" x 2½" rectangle. Make a total of 96 as shown.

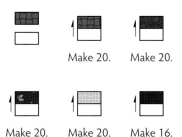

Make 20.   Make 20.

Make 20.   Make 20.   Make 16.

2. With right sides together, sew matching print 1½" x 2½" rectangles to the ends of a cream 2½" x 4½" rectangle. Make a total of 24 as shown.

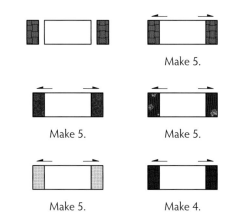

Make 5.

Make 5.   Make 5.

Make 5.   Make 4.

3. With right sides together, sew a cream 1½" x 2½" rectangle to each end of a print 2½" x 4½" rectangle. Make a total of 24 as shown.

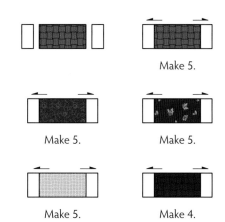

Make 5.

Make 5.   Make 5.

Make 5.   Make 4.

4. Using the same print throughout, lay out four print 2½" squares, two units from step 1, and one unit from step 2 in three rows as shown. Sew the pieces into rows. Sew the rows together to make an A block. Make a total of 24.

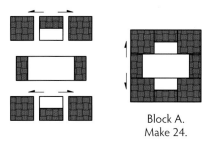

Block A.
Make 24.

5. Using the same print throughout, lay out four 2½" cream squares, two units from step 1, and one unit from step 3 in three rows as shown. Sew the pieces into rows. Sew the rows together to make a B block. Make a total of 24.

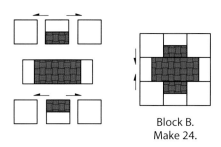

Block B.
Make 24.

Assembling the Quilt Top

1. Using a design wall or other flat surface, arrange the completed blocks into eight rows of six blocks each as shown above right.

2. Sew the blocks into rows, pressing the seam allowances toward the A blocks. Sew the rows together to form the quilt top. Press the seam allowances in one direction.

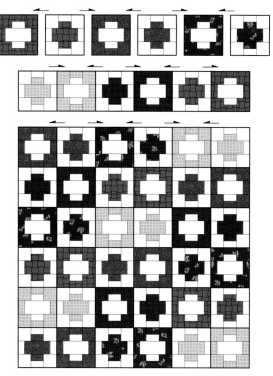

Quilt assembly

3. Referring to "Adding Borders" on page 62, sew two gold 2½" x 42" strips together to make one long strip; make two. Stitch the strips to the sides of the quilt top, and then trim the excess even with the top and bottom of the quilt top. Press the seam allowances toward the border strips. Sew the remaining gold strips to the top and bottom of the quilt. Trim the excess even with the sides of the quilt top. Press the seam allowances toward the strips.

4. Sew two black 6½"-wide strips together to make one long strip. Repeat to make four long strips. Sew the strips to the quilt top for the outer border. Press.

Finishing

1. Refer to "Completing the Quilt" on page 62 to layer the quilt top, batting, and backing. Quilt as desired.

2. Sew the black 2½"-wide strips together to form one continuous strip and use it to bind the quilt.

T-Ball

designed by Kathy Brown, pieced by Linda Reed, quilted by Carol Hilton

*O*h, how I love baseball! From my early years up to the present day, I've loved both watching the game and playing the game. One of my favorite pastimes today is attending our local university games every chance I get. Luckily for me, with the abundance of sports channels on television, I can even enjoy the excitement of the game in the comfort of my own home while stitching away on one quilt or another.

It was during the college world series this past year, watching my beloved Louisiana State University Tigers play, that the idea for this quilt was born. Although not sewn in the team's purple and gold fabrics, the inspiration behind the quilt remains the same!

You'll notice that I did something a little different in this quilt. Although I stayed with the concept of creating the blocks with five fat quarters, I liked two of the fabrics so much that I also used them for the outer border and the binding. If you want to do the same thing, just buy a fat quarter plus the border yardage of one fabric, and a fat quarter plus the binding yardage of another (in addition to the other three fat quarters and the white solid, of course).

So, why not stitch up your own version of "T-Ball"—perhaps in your school colors?

Finished quilt: 45½" x 53"
Finished block: 6" x 6"

Materials

Yardage is based on 42"-wide fabric. Fat quarters measure 18" x 21".

1 fat quarter *each* of citron, orange, and blue prints for blocks

1 fat quarter of light-orange dot for blocks

1 fat quarter of blue-and-orange floral for blocks

1½ yards of white solid for blocks and inner border

1 yard of coordinating fabric for outer border

½ yard of fabric for binding

3⅓ yards of fabric for backing

54" x 61" piece of batting

Cutting the Layered Fat Quarters

To cut the fat quarters efficiently, lay them all right side up, one on top of the other in a uniform stack (see "Rotary Cutting" on page 61). Trim the left and bottom edges of the stack to square them up. Refer to the cutting diagram below to cut the layered fabrics as indicated.

From *each* fat quarter, cut:

4 strips, 2" x 21"; crosscut into;
   12 squares, 2" x 2" (60 total)
   6 strips, 2" x 6½" (30 total)
2 strips, 3½" x 21"; crosscut into 6 rectangles,
   3½" x 5" (30 total)

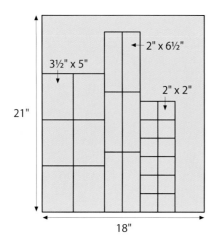

Cutting the Remaining Pieces

From the white solid, cut:

18 strips, 2" x 42"; crosscut *12 of the strips* into:
   60 strips, 2" x 5"
   24 strips, 2" x 6½"
5 strips, 2" x 36½"

From the outer-border fabric, cut:

8 strips, 3½" x 42"

From the binding fabric, cut:

6 strips, 2½" x 42"

Constructing the Blocks

All the blocks are made in the same manner. Press the seam allowances as indicated by the arrows in the diagrams.

1. Draw a diagonal line from corner to corner on the wrong side of two citron 2" squares.

2. Place a marked square on one end of a white 2" x 5" strip, right sides together with the diagonal line oriented as shown. Sew on the drawn line. Trim the excess ¼" from the sewn line, and fold back the triangle. Press. Make a second unit, this time with the diagonal line angled in the opposite direction. Sew on the drawn line, trim, and press as before.

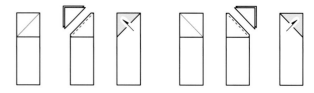

3. Orienting the units from step 2 as shown, sew them to opposite sides of a citron 3½" x 5" rectangle. Sew a citron 2" x 6½" strip to the top of the assembled unit to complete the block. Repeat steps 1-3 to make six blocks of each fat-quarter fabric, for a total of 30 blocks.

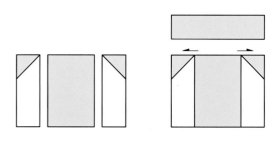

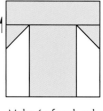

Make 6 of each color
(30 total).

Assembling the Quilt Top

1. Using a design wall or other flat surface, arrange the completed blocks in six rows of five blocks and four white 2" x 6½" sashing strips each as shown.

2. Sew the blocks and sashing strips into rows, and press the seam allowances toward the blocks. Sew the rows and the white 2" x 36½" sashing strips together to form the quilt top. Press the seam allowances toward the blocks.

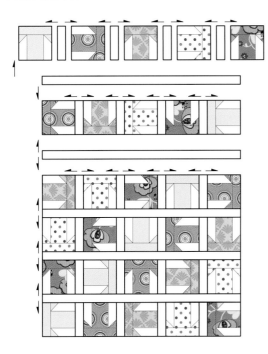

3. Referring to "Adding Borders" on page 62, sew two white 2" x 42" strips together to make one long strip. Make two. Stitch the strips to the sides of the quilt top, and then trim the excess even with the top and bottom of the quilt top. Press the seam allowances away from the strips. Sew the remaining white 2" x 42" strips to the top and bottom of the quilt. Trim the excess even with the sides of the quilt top. Press the seam allowances away from the strips

4. Sew two 3½"-wide outer-border strips together to make one long strip. Repeat to make four long strips. Sew the strips to the quilt top. Press the seam allowances toward the outer border.

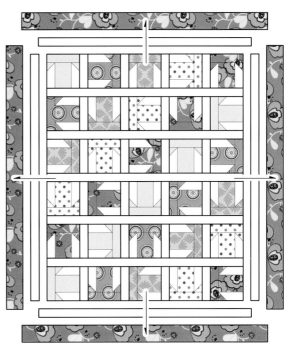

Quilt assembly

Finishing

1. Refer to "Completing the Quilt" on page 62 to layer the quilt top, batting, and backing. Quilt as desired.

2. Sew the 2½"-wide binding strips together to form one continuous strip and use it to bind the quilt.

Drop Box

designed by Kathy Brown, pieced by Linda Reed, quilted by Carol Hilton

*A*utumn has always been my favorite time of the year. Although in Louisiana the foliage doesn't undergo the dramatic changes of color that other areas of the country experience, we do see subtle shifts. When I was young and autumn would begin to approach, I'd pull out my trusty cigar box and go hunting. Leaves from the Chinese tallow tree in hues of red and orange were dropped into the box along with acorns and leaves from the oak trees, both brown and green. I guess in my childlike way, I was creating my own little version of autumn right there in my drop box!

The colors of fall are brought front and center in this simple but striking version of my long-ago drop box!

Finished quilt: 34½" x 48½"
Finished block: 6" x 6"

Materials

Yardage is based on 42"-wide fabric. Fat quarters measure 18" x 21".

1 fat quarter *each* of red, orange, brown, and green prints for blocks

1 fat quarter of black solid for blocks and pieced rectangles

1⅓ yards of tan solid for pieced rectangles, sashing, border, and binding

1¾ yards of fabric for backing

43" x 57" piece of batting

Cutting the Fat Quarters

To cut the red, orange, brown, and green fat quarters efficiently, lay them all right side up, one on top of the other in a uniform stack (see "Rotary Cutting" on page 61). Trim the left and bottom edges of the stack to square them up. Refer to the cutting diagrams at right and on page 42 to cut the layered fabrics and the black fat quarter as indicated.

From *each* red, orange, brown, and green fat quarter, cut:

6 strips, 2½" x 21"; crosscut into:
10 squares, 2½" x 2½" (40 total)
10 strips, 2½" x 6½" (40 total)

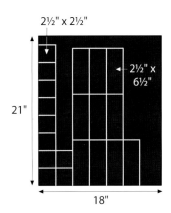

From the black fat quarter, cut:
6 strips, 2½" x 21"; crosscut into:
40 squares, 2½" x 2½"
4 rectangles, 2½" x 4½"

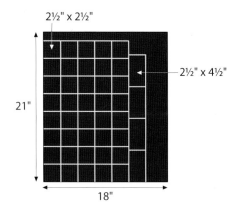

Cutting the Remaining Pieces

From the tan solid, cut on the *lengthwise* grain:
10 strips, 2½" x 44½"
4 strips, 2½" x 42"; crosscut into:
40 squares, 2½" x 2½"
8 rectangles, 2½" x 4½"

From the remaining tan solid, cut on the *crosswise* grain:
2 strips, 2½" x 34½"

Constructing the Blocks and Pieced Rectangles

All the blocks are made in the same manner. Press the seam allowances as indicated by the arrows in the diagrams.

1. Sew two tan 2½" squares to opposite sides of a black 2½" square to make a small pieced rectangle; make 20. Press. Sew two tan 2½" x 4½" rectangles to opposite sides of a black 2½" x 4½" rectangle to make a large pieced rectangle; make four. Press.

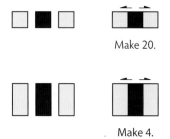

Make 20.

Make 4.

2. Sew two red 2½" squares to opposite sides of a black 2½" square to make a pieced strip. Sew the pieced strip and two red 2½" x 6½" strips together as shown to complete a block. Repeat to make five blocks of each color, for a total of 20 blocks.

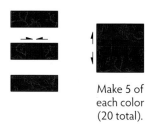

Make 5 of each color (20 total).

Assembling the Quilt Top

1. Using a design wall or other flat surface, arrange the completed blocks and pieced rectangles in four vertical columns of five blocks, five pieced rectangles, and one large pieced rectangle each, as shown in the quilt assembly diagram.

2. Sew the blocks and pieced rectangles into columns. Sew five of the tan 2½" x 44½" strips and the columns together. Sew the tan 2½" x 34½" strips to the top and bottom of the quilt.

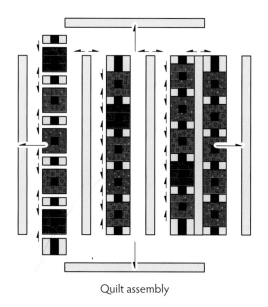

Quilt assembly

Finishing

1. Refer to "Completing the Quilt" on page 62 to layer the quilt top, batting, and backing. Quilt as desired.

2. Sew the remaining tan 2½"-wide strips together to form one continuous strip and use it to bind the quilt.

Black Tie Affair

designed by Kathy Brown, pieced by Linda Reed, quilted by Carol Hilton

*O*ur family was big on traditions when I was growing up. One special and favorite tradition was grounded in teaching my two brothers and me how to behave in social situations when we were very young (aka, how not to embarrass your parents in a fancy restaurant). A couple times a year, we would get dressed in our Sunday best, pile into the Rambler station wagon, and head for an unfamiliar restaurant. There we would be faced with crystal goblets, china, and more cutlery than we knew what to do with. Getting to act like the grownups, we were allowed to order Shirley Temples (kid-friendly nonalcoholic drinks made of ginger ale or lemon-lime soda and grenadine or cherries) and whatever we wanted for dinner—a huge treat back in the day!

When I happened across this grouping of black prints, I knew exactly what I wanted to make with them: a simple yet elegant quilt, one that is surely fitting for a "Black Tie Affair" and a remembrance of those special family outings!

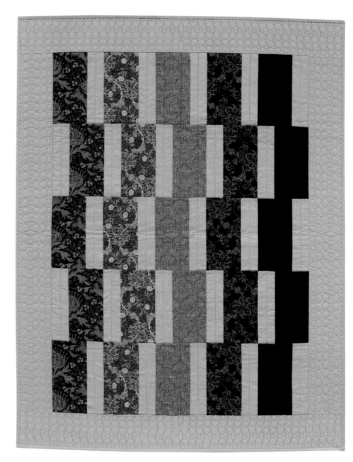

Finished quilt: 38½" x 48½"
Finished block: 6" x 8"

Materials

Yardage is based on 42"-wide fabric. Fat quarters measure 18" x 21".

1 fat quarter *each* of 5 assorted deep gray and black prints for blocks

2 yards of gray solid for blocks, border, and binding

2⅞ yards of fabric for backing

47" x 57" piece of batting

Cutting the Layered Fat Quarters

To cut the fat quarters efficiently, lay them all right side up, one on top of the other in a uniform stack (see "Rotary Cutting" on page 61). Trim the left and bottom edges of the stack to square them up. Refer to the cutting diagram below to cut the layered fabrics as indicated.

From *each* fat quarter, cut:

3 strips, 4½" x 21"; crosscut into 5 rectangles, 4½" x 8½" (25 total)

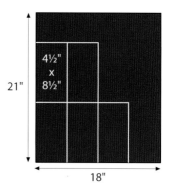

Cutting the Remaining Pieces

From the gray solid, cut:
   12 strips 2½" x 42"; crosscut *7 of the strips* into 25
      strips, 2½" x 8½"
   4 strips, 4½" x 42"

Constructing the Blocks

Sew a gray-solid 2½" x 8½" strip and a print
4½" x 8½" rectangle together as shown. Press the
seam allowances away from the gray strip. Repeat
to make 25 blocks.

Make 25.

Assembling the Quilt Top

1. Using a design wall or other flat surface,
   arrange the completed blocks in five rows of
   five blocks each, orienting the blocks as shown
   in the quilt assembly diagram.

2. Sew the blocks into rows, pressing the seam
   allowances away from the gray-solid strips.
   Sew the rows together to form the quilt top.
   Press the seam allowances in one direction.

3. Referring to "Adding Borders" on page 62, sew
   two gray 4½"-wide strips to the sides of the
   quilt top, and then trim the excess even with
   the top and bottom of the quilt top. Press the

seam allowances toward the border strips. Sew
the remaining gray 4½"-wide strips to the top
and bottom of the quilt. Trim the excess even
with the sides of the quilt top. Press the seam
allowances toward the strips.

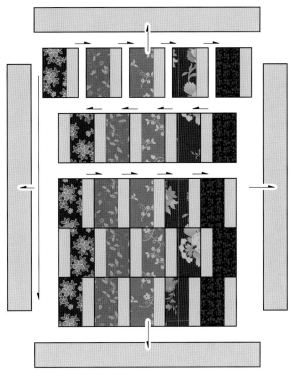

Quilt assembly

Finishing

1. Refer to "Completing the Quilt" on page 62 to
   layer the quilt top, batting, and backing. Quilt
   as desired.

2. Sew the gray 2½"-wide strips together to
   form one continuous strip and use it to bind
   the quilt.

Be It Ever So Humble

designed by Kathy Brown, pieced by Linda Reed, quilted by Carol Hilton

There's a long-standing myth in the quilting world that goes something like this: Traditionally, quilters made one intentional mistake in every quilt, whether it was using a different color in a block, turning a quilt block the wrong way, alternating placement of a block, or other scenarios. The theory is, because only God is perfect, no one should attempt to make a perfect quilt, so women supposedly included a humility block in all of their quilts. Whether or not this was an actual quiltmaking practice, or just a wee bit of fun to cover up one's mistakes, I thought it would be fun to include a humility block in this quilt. Can you find it?

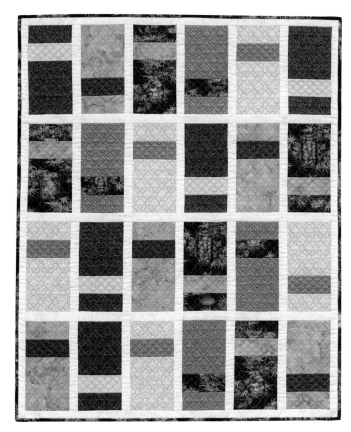

Finished quilt: 37½" x 45½"
Finished block: 5" x 10"

Materials

Yardage is based on 42"-wide fabric. Fat quarters measure 18" x 21".

1 fat quarter *each* of brown, tan, dark-brown, blue, and cream prints for blocks

1 yard of cream solid for sashing and border

½ yard of fabric for binding*

2⅞ yards of fabric for backing

46" x 54" piece of batting

In the quilt shown, the binding is made from the same dark-brown print used in the blocks.

Cutting the Fat Quarters

To cut the brown, tan, dark-brown, and cream fat quarters efficiently, lay them all right side up, one on top of the other in a uniform stack (see "Rotary Cutting" on page 61). Trim the left and bottom edges of the stack to square them up. Refer to the cutting diagram at right and on page 48 to cut the layered fabrics and the blue fat quarter as indicated.

From *each* brown, tan, dark-brown, and cream fat quarter, cut:

  3 strips, 5½" x 21"; crosscut into:
    10 strips, 2½" x 5½" (40 total; 1 dark-brown strip will be extra)
    5 rectangles, 5½" x 6½" (20 total)

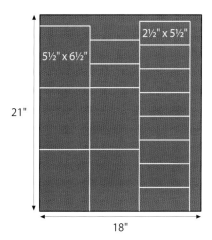

From the blue fat quarter, cut:
3 strips, 5½" x 21"; crosscut into:
   9 strips, 2½" x 5½"
   4 rectangles, 5½" x 6½"

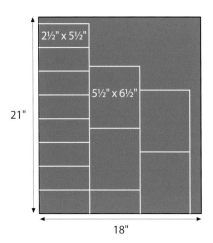

Cutting the Remaining Pieces

From the cream solid, cut:
13 strips, 1½" x 42"; crosscut *7 of these strips* into:
   20 strips, 1½" x 10½"
3 strips, 1½" x 35½"

From the binding fabric, cut:
5 strips, 2½" x 42"

Constructing the Blocks

All the blocks are made in the same manner. Press the seam allowances as indicated by the arrows in the diagrams.

Sew a tan 2½" x 5½" strip and a brown 2½" x 5½" strip together. Sew a brown 5½" x 6½" rectangle to the bottom of this unit to complete the block. Repeat to make a total of 24 blocks in the fabric combinations shown.

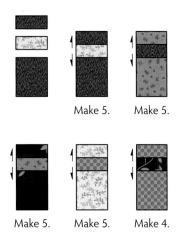

Make 5.   Make 5.

Make 5.   Make 5.   Make 4.

Assembling the Quilt Top

1. Using a design wall or other flat surface, arrange the completed blocks and the cream 1½" x 10½" strips into four rows of six blocks and five strips each, orienting the blocks as shown in the quilt assembly diagram.

2. Sew the blocks and strips into rows, pressing the seam allowances toward the blocks. Sew the rows and the cream 1½" x 35½" strips together to form the quilt top. Press the seam allowances toward the rows.

3. Referring to "Adding Borders" on page 62, sew two cream 1½" x 42" strips together to make one long strip; make two. Stitch the strips to the sides of the quilt top, and then trim the excess even with the top and bottom of the quilt top. Press the seam allowances toward the border strips. Sew the remaining cream 1½" x 42" strips to the top and bottom of the quilt. Trim the excess even with the sides of the quilt top. Press the seam allowances toward the strips.

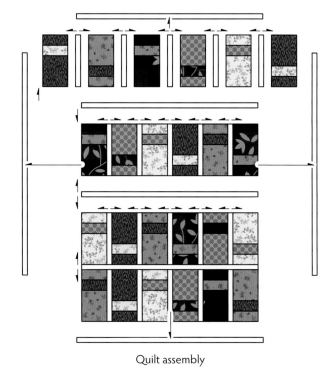

Quilt assembly

Finishing

1. Refer to "Completing the Quilt" on page 62 to layer the quilt top, batting, and backing. Quilt as desired.

2. Sew the 2½"-wide binding strips together to form one continuous strip and use it to bind the quilt.

Farmhouse Favorite

designed by Kathy Brown, pieced by Linda Reed, quilted by Carol Hilton

*W*hen I was a child, one of my favorite places to be was at my great-aunt and -uncle's farm. With all of the horses, chickens, and cattle, there was never a dull moment. I have such sweet memories of waking up early in the morning in the big Civil War–era bed, snuggled under the weight of a hand-stitched quilt, and then running into the kitchen to "help" my great-aunt make breakfast. Everything was prepared on the well-worn and much-loved farmhouse table. The table and benches, made from hand-hewn cypress, were the focal point of the kitchen and everything that happened within.

To this day, I still dream of having a kitchen large enough to accommodate a farmhouse table like my great-aunt's where a lifetime of memories could be forged. Perhaps one day that will happen, and this very table runner will have its home!

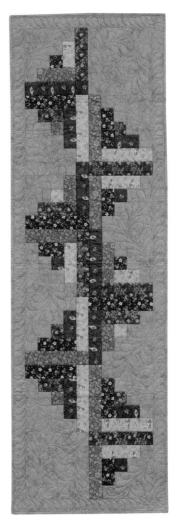

Finished quilt: 24½" x 74½"
Finished block: 10" x 10"

Materials

Yardage is based on 42"-wide fabric. Fat quarters measure 18" x 21".

1 fat quarter *each* of blue, red, brown, green, and tan prints for blocks

1⅞ yards of gold solid for blocks, border, and binding

2½ yards of fabric for backing

33" x 83" piece of batting

Cutting the Layered Fat Quarters

To cut the fat quarters efficiently, lay them all right side up, one on top of the other in a uniform stack (see "Rotary Cutting" on page 61). Trim the left and bottom edges of the stack to square them up. Refer to the cutting diagram at right to cut the layered fabrics as indicated.

From *each* fat quarter, cut:

6 strips, 2½" x 21"; crosscut into:
    3 squares, 2½" x 2½" (15 total; 3 will be extra)
    3 strips, 2½" x 4½" (15 total; 3 will be extra)
    3 strips, 2½" x 6½" (15 total; 3 will be extra)
    3 strips, 2½" x 8½" (15 total; 3 will be extra)
    3 strips, 2½" x 10½" (15 total; 3 will be extra)

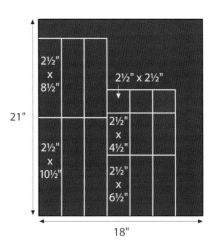

Cutting the Remaining Pieces

From the gold solid, cut:
  20 strips, 2½" x 42"; crosscut *8 of the strips* into:
    12 squares, 2½" x 2½"
    12 strips, 2½" x 4½"
    12 strips, 2½" x 6½"
    12 strips, 2½" x 8½"
  2 squares, 10½" x 10½"

Constructing the Blocks

This table runner is composed of Log Cabin blocks stitched in five different color combinations to make the best use of your fat quarters. Press the seam allowances as indicated by the arrows in the diagrams.

Block A

Sew a blue 2½" square to the bottom of a gold 4½" strip. Add a gold 6½" strip to the right as shown. Sew a tan 4½" strip to the bottom. Add a gold 8½" strip to the right as shown. Sew a gold 2½" square to the top of a green 6½" strip; sew it to the left side as shown. Sew a brown 8½" strip to the bottom. Sew a red 10½" strip to the left to complete block A. Make two.

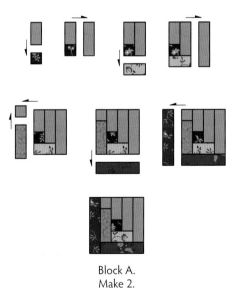

Block A.
Make 2.

Block B

Sew a red 2½" square to the bottom of a gold 4½" strip. Add a gold 6½" strip to the right as shown. Sew a blue 4½" strip to the bottom. Add a gold 8½" strip to the right as shown. Sew a gold 2½" square to the top of a tan 6½" strip; sew it to the left side as shown. Sew a green 8½" strip to the bottom. Sew a brown 10½" strip to the left to complete block B. Make three.

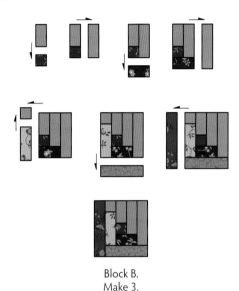

Block B.
Make 3.

Block C

Sew a brown 2½" square to the bottom of a gold 4½" strip. Add a gold 6½" strip to the right as shown. Sew a red 4½" strip to the bottom. Add a gold 8½" strip to the right as shown. Sew a gold 2½" square to the top of a blue 6½" strip; sew it to the left side as shown. Sew a tan 8½" strip to the bottom. Sew a green 10½" strip to the left to complete block C. Make three.

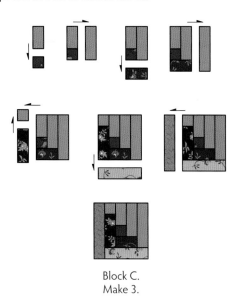

Block C.
Make 3.

Block D

Sew a green 2½" square to the bottom of a gold 4½" strip. Add a gold 6½" strip to the right as shown. Sew a brown 4½" strip to the bottom. Add a gold 8½" strip to the right as shown. Sew a gold 2½" square to the top of a red 6½" strip; sew it to the left side as shown. Sew a blue 8½" strip to the bottom. Sew a tan 10½" strip to the left to complete block D. Make two.

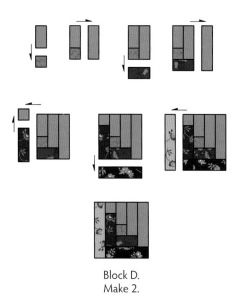

Block D.
Make 2.

Block E

Sew a tan 2½" square to the bottom of a gold 4½" strip. Add a gold 6½" strip to the right as shown. Sew a green 4½" strip to the bottom. Add a gold 8½" strip to the right as shown. Sew a gold 2½" square to the top of a brown 6½" strip; sew it to the left side as shown. Sew a red 8½" strip to the bottom. Sew a blue 10½" strip to the left to complete block E. Make two.

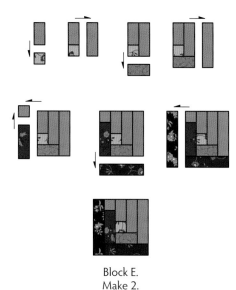

Block E.
Make 2.

Assembling the Quilt Top

1. Using a design wall or other flat surface, arrange the completed blocks and gold 10½" squares into seven rows as shown in the quilt assembly diagram.

2. Sew the blocks into rows, pressing the seam allowances in opposite directions from row to row. Sew the rows together to form the quilt top. Press the seam allowances in one direction.

3. Referring to "Adding Borders" on page 62, sew two gold 2½" x 42" strips together to make one long strip; make two. Stitch the strips to the sides of the quilt top, and then trim the excess even with the top and bottom of the quilt top. Press the seam allowances toward the border strips. Sew the remaining pieced gold 2½" x 42" strips to the top and bottom of the quilt. Trim the excess even with the sides of the quilt top. Press the seam allowances toward the strips.

Finishing

1. Refer to "Completing the Quilt" on page 62 to layer the quilt top, batting, and backing. Quilt as desired.

2. Sew the remaining six gold 2½"-wide strips together to form one continuous strip and use it to bind the quilt.

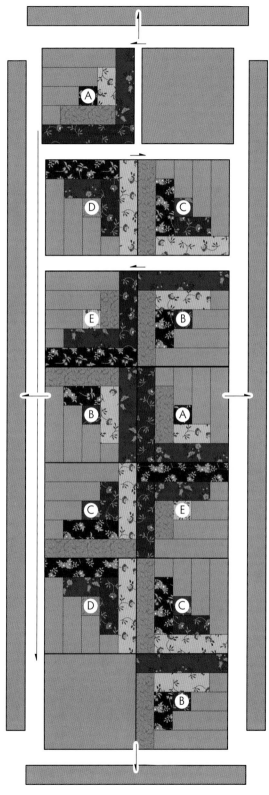

Quilt assembly

Confetti

designed by Kathy Brown, pieced by Linda Reed, quilted by Carol Hilton

*M*y love of color is widely known throughout my circle of family and friends. Sometimes it's been a good thing, other times—well, not so much! As a child I could always be found with my crayons, coloring books, colored construction paper, scissors, and glue, creating something—anything—in color!

One time I took my trusty scissors and a few sheets of brightly colored construction paper and set my mind to creating the beautiful confetti that I saw raining down on the Macy's Thanksgiving Day parade! I worked diligently, filling an envelope with minute squares of rainbow-hued paper. But I neglected to tell my mom what was in the envelope, or—for that matter—even seal the envelope. What started out as a fun project quickly developed into a huge mess sprinkled all over my mom's freshly mopped and waxed kitchen floor. I spent the better part of that Thanksgiving afternoon scraping up bits of confetti. Needless to say this was one of those "not so much" times! I think this *version of confetti is one that my mom could certainly appreciate.*

Materials

Yardage is based on 42"-wide fabric. Fat quarters measure 18" x 21".

1 fat quarter *each* of orange, yellow, blue, and green prints for blocks

1 fat quarter of multicolored stripe for blocks

4⅜ yards of white solid for blocks, background, and borders

⅔ yard of fabric for binding*

4⅝ yards of fabric for backing

75" x 81" piece of batting

In the quilt shown, the binding is made from the same multicolored stripe used in the blocks.

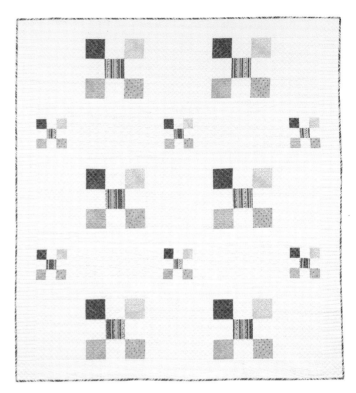

Finished quilt: 66½" x 72½"
Finished blocks: 12" x 12" and 6" x 6"

Cutting the Layered Fat Quarters

To cut the fat quarters efficiently, lay them all right side up, one on top of the other in a uniform stack (see "Rotary Cutting" on page 61). Trim the left and bottom edges of the stack to square them up. Refer to the cutting diagram below to cut the layered fabrics as indicated.

From *each* fat quarter, cut:
2 strips, 4½" x 21"; crosscut into 6 squares, 4½" x 4½" (30 total)
1 strip, 2½" x 21"; crosscut into 6 squares, 2½" x 2½" (30 total)

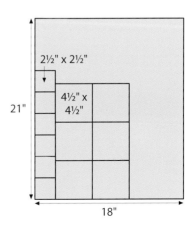

Cutting the Remaining Pieces

From the white solid, cut:
  1 strip, 14½" x 42"; crosscut into 3 rectangles, 12½" x 14½"
  2 strips, 2½" x 42"; crosscut into 24 squares, 2½" x 2½"
  19 strips, 4½" x 42"; crosscut 3 of the strips into 24 squares, 4½" x 4½"
  2 strips, 10½" x 42"; crosscut into 6 rectangles, 10½" x 12½"
  2 strips, 6½" x 42"; crosscut into 4 strips, 6½" x 20½"

From the binding fabric, cut:
  8 strips, 2½" x 42"

Constructing the Blocks

All the blocks are made in the same manner. Press the seam allowances as indicated by the arrows in the diagrams.

Large Nine Patch Block

Lay out one 4½" square from each fat quarter and four white 4½" squares in three rows as shown. Sew the squares into rows. Sew the rows together to complete a large Nine Patch block. Repeat to make a total of six blocks.

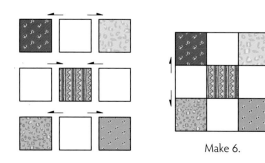

Make 6.

Small Nine Patch Block

Lay out one 2½" square from each fat quarter and four white 2½" squares in three rows as shown. Sew the squares into rows. Sew the rows together to complete a small Nine Patch block. Repeat to make a total of six blocks.

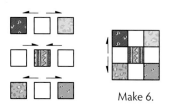

Make 6.

Assembling the Quilt Top

1. Sew two white 4½" x 42" strips together to make one long strip; make four. Trim the strips to 4½" x 58½".

2. Using a design wall or other flat surface, arrange the large Nine Patch blocks and the white 10½" x 12½" and 12½" x 14½" rectangles into three rows as shown in the quilt assembly diagram. Arrange the small Nine Patch blocks and the white 6½" x 20½" strips into two rows as shown. Sew the block rows and the white 4½" x 58½" strips together to form the quilt top. Press.

3. Referring to "Adding Borders" on page 62, sew two white 4½" x 42" strips together to make one long strip; make four. Stitch two of the strips to the sides of the quilt top, and then trim the excess even with the top and bottom of the quilt top. Press the seam allowances toward the border strips. Sew the remaining long strips to the top and bottom of the quilt. Trim the excess even with the sides of the quilt top; press as for the side borders.

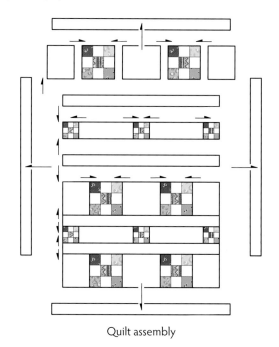

Quilt assembly

Finishing

1. Refer to "Completing the Quilt" on page 62 to layer the quilt top, batting, and backing. Quilt as desired.

2. Sew the 2½"-wide binding strips together to form one continuous strip and use it to bind the quilt.

Tranquillity

designed by Kathy Brown, pieced by Linda Reed, quilted by Carol Hilton

A few years ago I had the opportunity to travel to Iowa. My husband was born in Des Moines, and I was excited to see the state that he so fondly remembered from his childhood. While there, I stopped in the town of Garner to visit Country Threads Quilt Shop—a visit that was at the top of my bucket list! I'm a true farm girl at heart, and Country Threads was everything I dreamed it would be. From the chickens and the goats to the cats and the dogs, I was in heaven with the surroundings, not to mention the quilt shop and its fabulous staff and owners! Trekking up the stairs to the hayloft to see all the quilts on display was a special treat in itself. As I exited the hayloft onto the outdoor landing, I was awed by the horizon that greeted me—a sea of golden corn as far as I could see, and storm clouds approaching in the distance. I was overcome with such a sense of tranquillity, I just knew in my heart that this was true paradise. When I found the fabrics for this quilt, I knew they would be transformed into a tangible memory of the Iowa countryside and the beauty I found that day! So much so, in fact, that I sort of "broke the rules" to make this quilt. Instead of purchasing just one fat quarter each of the five fabrics, I bought two of each! By doing this, I was able to make a quilt big enough to cover my bed, and bring my memories to life each and every day. I'm sure you won't mind breaking the rules just this once so that you, too, can have a wonderful bed-sized quilt.

Finished quilt: 84¼" x 98⅜"
Finished block: 10" x 10"

Materials

Yardage is based on 42"-wide fabric. Fat quarters measure 18" x 21".

2 fat quarters *each* of 5 assorted blue and brown batiks for blocks

8⅛ yards of light-yellow tone on tone for blocks, setting triangles, and border

⅞ yard of fabric for binding

8½ yards of fabric for backing

93" x 107" piece of batting

Cutting the Layered Fat Quarters

To cut the fat quarters efficiently, lay them all right side up, one on top of the other in a uniform stack (see "Rotary Cutting" on page 61). Trim the left and bottom edges of the stack to square them up. Refer to the cutting diagram on page 59 to cut the layered fabrics as indicated.

From *each* fat quarter, cut:
  5 strips, 3½" x 21"; crosscut into 25 squares,
    3½" x 3½" (50 squares total per fabric)

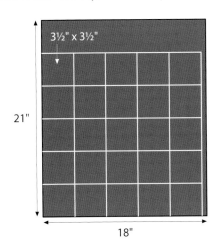

Cutting the Remaining Pieces

From the light-yellow tone-on-tone, cut:
  23 strips, 3½" x 42"; crosscut into 250 squares,
    3½" x 3½"
  22 strips, 3" x 42"; crosscut into:
    50 squares, 3" x 3"
    50 rectangles, 3" x 5½"
    50 rectangles, 3" x 8"
  5 squares, 15½" x 15½"; cut each square into
    quarters diagonally to yield 20 side setting
    triangles (2 will be extra)
  2 squares, 8" x 8"; cut each square in half diago-
    nally to yield 4 corner setting triangles
  9 strips, 7" x 42"

From the binding fabric, cut:
  10 strips, 2½" x 42"

Constructing the Blocks

Each block uses two half-square-triangle units
from each of the five batiks. To give this quilt its
scrappy look, sew the half-square-triangle units
together in a random fashion, without sewing
two like-fabric triangles together. All blocks are
sewn in the same manner. Press the seam allowances as indicated by the arrows in the diagrams.

1. Draw a diagonal line from corner to corner on
   the wrong side of the yellow 3½" squares.

2. Place a marked square and a batik square right
   sides together. Sew ¼" from the marked line on
   each side. Cut on the drawn line to yield two
   half-square-triangle units. Repeat to make 100
   half-square-triangle units from *each* of the five
   batik fabrics. Trim the units to measure 3" x 3".

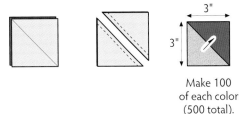

Make 100
of each color
(500 total).

3. Arrange 10 half-square-triangle units, one
   yellow 3" square, one yellow 3" x 5½" rectangle,
   and one yellow 3" x 8" rectangle into four rows
   as shown. Sew the pieces into rows, and then
   sew the rows together to complete the block.
   Make a total of 50 blocks.

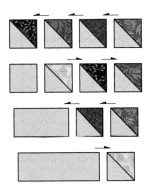

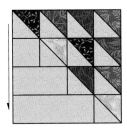

Make 50.

Assembling the Quilt Top

1. Using a design wall or other flat surface, arrange the completed blocks in diagonal rows with the yellow side setting triangles and corner setting triangles as shown in the quilt assembly diagram.

2. Sew the blocks and side setting triangles into diagonal rows. Press the seam allowances as shown. Sew the rows together and add the corner triangles last.

3. Referring to "Adding Borders" on page 62, sew three yellow 7"-wide strips together to make one long strip. Repeat to make three long strips. Stitch two of the strips to the sides of the quilt top, and then trim the excess even with the top and bottom of the quilt top. Press the

seam allowances toward the border strips. Sew the remaining long strip to the top of the quilt. Trim the excess even with the sides of the quilt top. Press the seam allowance toward the strip. The bottom row of blocks combines with setting triangles to give the illusion of a border strip on the bottom of the quilt.

Finishing

1. Refer to "Completing the Quilt" on page 62 to layer the quilt top, batting, and backing. Quilt as desired.

2. Sew the 2½"-wide binding strips together to form one continuous strip and use it to bind the quilt.

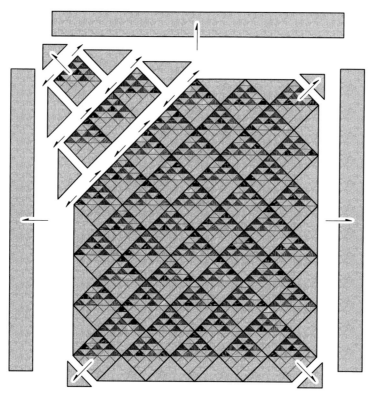

Quilt assembly

Creating successful Take 5 quilts requires a few basic supplies and a familiarity with simple quilting techniques. Follow the guidelines throughout this section as you construct your quilts.

Materials

If you're already a quilter, you probably have most of these tools and supplies on hand. If you're new to quilting, these basic items will be enough to get started.

- Good-quality, 100% cotton fabrics
- Thread in a neutral color
- Rotary cutter
- 24" x 36" or larger rotary-cutting mat
- 6½" x 24½" acrylic ruler
- Self-adhesive ruler grip dots or Invisi-Grip (to keep your ruler from slipping)
- Glass-head silk pins
- Seam ripper
- A sewing machine in good working order with a ¼" presser foot

Rotary Cutting

Since rotary cutting is a topic covered in so many quilting books, I won't go into great detail about how to use a rotary cutter, except for how to cut layered fat quarters. What you do need to remember as you begin each new project in this book is to start with a new rotary-cutter blade. You will be cutting through multiple layers of fabric and will need the sharp, accurate edge that a new blade provides.

1. To rotary-cut fat quarters, open each one and press out any creases. I prefer to starch the fabrics at this time so that I get a more accurate cut, but this is a personal preference.

2. Lay each fat quarter down on your cutting mat, one on top of the other and with the selvages all closest to you. Place one 21" edge on the left and the other 21" edge on the right. Lay the 6½" x 24½" ruler over the left edge. Check

to make sure that all layers of fabric are showing underneath the ruler and that you'll be trimming off all of the edges.

3. Using a rotary cutter, cut along the right edge of the ruler. Discard the cut-off edges.

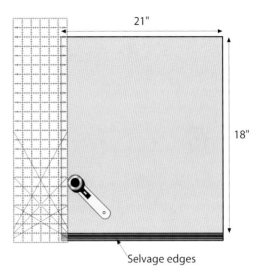

21"

18"

Selvage edges

4. Rotate the fat quarters or reposition your body so that the newly cut edge is closest to you and the selvages are to your right. Align the short end of the ruler with the straightened edge of the fabric stack, and again check to make sure that all layers of fabric are visible before cutting. Using a rotary cutter, trim off all of the selvages and discard.

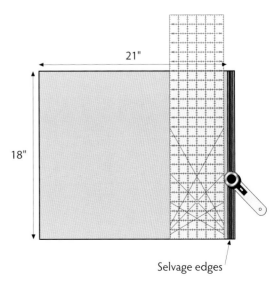

21"

18"

Selvage edges

5. Having made these edges square, you're ready to begin cutting your fat quarters. Follow the cutting diagrams included in each quilt project to make the individual cuts. If necessary, repeat steps 2 and 3 to restraighten the edges after you've made several cuts, or if the layers shift while cutting.

Pinning and Pressing

To pin or not to pin is an issue that most quilters face in their quilting journey. I have found through much trial, error, and angst that it's far better to take the time to pin. Your blocks will be more likely to go together with accurate intersecting points, and you'll avoid ripping the blocks apart later when they don't fit together properly. If you opt not to pin, that's your personal choice, but don't say I didn't urge you to do so!

Accurate pressing is a must in my opinion. As with pinning, I find that my blocks fit together better and are much straighter if I press each seam after sewing it. The instructions for each project will indicate the proper pressing direction for seam allowances at every step of the process; follow these recommendations carefully for best results.

Adding Borders

All of the quilts in this book feature borders with simple butted corners—no mitering or complex measuring is involved. Cut border strips across the width of the fabric and piece them when needed to achieve the required length.

To piece the border strips, place the ends of the strips right sides together at right angles as shown. Sew diagonally from the point where the strips meet at the top of the horizontal strip to the point where the strips meet at the bottom of the horizontal strip. Trim ¼" from the stitching line and press the seam allowances open.

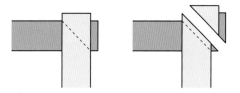

To add the borders to the quilt, mark the center points of each edge of the quilt top. Mark the center point on one long edge of each border strip. With right sides together, pin the left and right border strips to the quilt top, matching the center marks. There will be excess border fabric extending beyond the quilt top. Stitch the borders in place, and then trim the excess even with the top and bottom of the quilt top. Press the seam allowances toward the border strips. Repeat for the top and bottom borders, trimming the excess even with the sides of the quilt top.

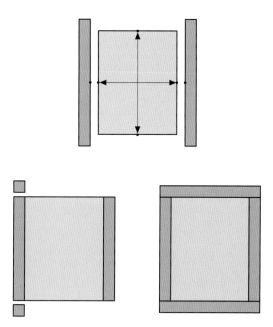

Completing the Quilt

When the quilt top is pieced, you can move on to the final steps of finishing your quilt.

Layering and Quilting

Before the quilting begins, prepare the backing and batting so that they're at least 4" wider and longer than the quilt top. The fabric requirements in each project have allowed for this excess. Layer the batting between the backing and the quilt top, and baste the layers together with pins for machine quilting or thread for hand quilting. Quilt as desired.

All of the quilts in this book were quilted on a long-arm quilting machine, but you can certainly use any quilting method that you prefer. If someone else will be doing the quilting, be sure to check with the quilter regarding the backing size and preparation of your quilt top.

Binding

I used traditional double-fold binding for all of the quilts in this book. I make a continuous length of binding with strips that are cut 2½" wide. All yardage amounts are based on 2½"-wide strips cut across the width of the fabric, except where fat quarters are used for the binding strips.

1. Join binding strips with a diagonal seam, in the same manner as for border strips (see page 62), to make one long strip.

2. Press the binding strip in half lengthwise with wrong sides together.

3. Leaving an 8" to 10" tail at the beginning, sew the binding to the quilt top using a ¼" seam allowance. Stop stitching ⅜" from the first corner and miter the corners as shown.

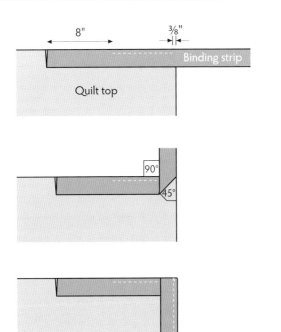

4. Stop sewing when you're about 12" from the beginning; backstitch. Overlap the end of the strip with the beginning tail. Trim the end of the binding strip so that it overlaps by 2½" (or the width that you cut your binding). Place the binding ends together at right angles and sew the ends together on the diagonal as shown. Trim, leaving a ¼" seam allowance. Press the seam allowances open. Reposition the binding on the quilt and finish sewing.

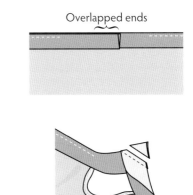

Overlapped ends

Unstitched quilt edge

5. Fold the binding to the back of the quilt and hand stitch it in place, mitering the corners. For ease of folding the binding over, I add spray starch to the binding and press it toward the raw edges of the quilt.

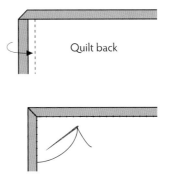

Quilt back

About the Author

It's hard to believe that 20 years ago I walked into a quilt shop and knew instantly that I'd found the answer my creative soul had been searching for. Among all of the fabric, threads, paint, pins, needles, rulers, and everything else that encompasses my quilting world, I am at my happiest. As I have said many times before, I'm the luckiest girl in the world. With this job that fulfills me creatively, a family who loves and supports me, my mini zoo of dogs and cats that love me unconditionally, and the best of friends surrounding me—I know in my heart just how blessed I am. I get to wake each and every day knowing that I'm living my dream of loving my life *and* my work, and who could ask for more than that?

Acknowledgments

With a grateful heart, I give warm thanks to:

My BFFs forever: Linda Reed, Paula Toups, Carol Hilton, Debbie Field, Tara Darr, and Debbie Bamber—friends from the start, sisters in my heart.

Red Rooster Fabrics: Anna and Carol. You work diligently to bring my ideas into artful elegance through my fabric designs, and I am forever honored to be one of your designers.

The quilters and quilt-shop owners who buy my patterns, books, and fabrics: you continue to let me live my dream of loving my work by supporting my efforts. I'm honored that you consider my efforts worthy of your time and patronage.

And last but not least, the fabulous staff at Martingale for their faith in me once again! Y'all are truly the best!